4D LOVE

The Extravagance of God's Love and Experiencing It

ISBN-13: 9798224879922

Cover design by: Nikki Garcia
Copyright Case Number: 1-13514677331
Printed in the United States of America

DEDICATION

This book is dedicated firstly to my Lord and savior Jesus Christ. I love Him IMMENSELY!!! Next, to my husband and 4 beautiful children. Finally, to all of those who are consistently laying down their will for the will of God. Love is sacrificial and not always easy but absolutely necessary.

READER'S TESTIMONIAL

For me personally, this book is an eye-opener regarding the Bible verse 1 Corinthians 13:1, as it explicitly expresses the impact of love in a more dynamic way. I truly commend your remarkable effort in crafting this wonderful piece. It is engaging, unambiguous, and enlightening. I felt blessed reading every bit of it. May God shower you with even greater insights and fortify your strength.

- Celeste

TABLE OF CONTENTS

INTRODUCTION THE ALTAR OF GOD AND MAN

The purpose of this introduction is to establish the foundation for the revelation presented in this book.

Have you ever considered that we are altars? Or have you ever read in the Bible that the cross was an altar and Jesus was a living sacrifice? The Bible states that our bodies are the temple of God (1 Corinthians 6:19-20). We are living, breathing tabernacles. We carry the presence of God inside of us. But have you ever considered that our **soul** is a sacrifice on our altar?

Genesis 2:7 states that God breathed breath into man and he became a **living soul**.

Consider the fact that Jesus, the living soul, was a living sacrifice. I believe that makes it safe to surmise that all of Jesus' motives, emotions, conscious and unconscious thinking, actions, and feelings were burning as incense on the altar, rendering sacrifices unto the Lord.

Opening this thought up further, Ephesians 1:7-10 in the MSG Bible states, "Because of the sacrifice of the Messiah, his blood poured out on the **altar of the Cross**, we're a free people—free of penalties and punishments chalked up by all our misdeeds. And not just barely free, either. Abundantly free! He thought of everything, provided for everything we could possibly need, letting us in on the plans he took such delight in making. He set it all out before us in Christ, a long-range plan in which everything would be brought together and summed up in him, everything in deepest heaven, everything on planet earth."

To reiterate, **the cross was an altar**, as seen in the scripture above. When we receive the Holy Spirit, then we too become a living tabernacle just like Jesus. We house His presence on the inside of us, and we become an altar and a sacrifice all at the same time. Isn't that amazing!

Leviticus 17:11 affirms this.
"For the life of the flesh is in the blood, and I have given it to you upon the **altar to make atonement for your souls**; for it is the **blood that makes atonement for the soul.**".

Our Lord and Savior, Jesus Christ, was the perfect sacrifice and became our High Priest after the order of Melchizedek. Because of His blood, our souls are atoned for.

Another thing to bring into consideration is that, just as the cross was an altar, it also had **length, depth, breadth, and height**—the four dimensions of love. We see this even when Solomon offered 1000 offerings on the altar at the high place of Gibeon. The altar there was built from shittim wood overlaid with brass, and it had depth, length, height, and breadth.

From the scripture below, we see that God told Moses to have Israel bring Him offerings, and God expressed to him how to build the tabernacle.

Exodus 27:1-2

> **1** *And thou shalt make an altar of shittim wood, five cubits long, and five cubits broad; the altar shall be foursquare: and the height thereof shall be three cubits.*

> **2** *And thou shalt make the horns of it upon the four corners thereof: his horns shall be of the same: and thou shalt overlay it with brass.*

The scripture below now shows how Solomon in turn offered offerings on the altar.

1 Kings 1:3-5

3 And Solomon loved the Lord, walking in the statutes of David his father: only he sacrificed and burnt incense in high places.

4 And the king went to Gibeon to sacrifice there; for that was the great high place: a thousand burnt offerings did Solomon offer upon that altar.

5 In Gibeon the Lord appeared to Solomon in a dream by night: and God said, Ask what I shall give thee.

In the scriptures above, we see that because Solomon loved the Lord so much, he made

1000 burnt offering sacrifices on the altar before the Lord. Solomon poured out his love for God in worship, and God's response to that worship was His presence. God came to see about holy and acceptable offerings before Him.

The sacrifice of Jesus was His life on the cross, and our lives are also a daily sacrifice unto the Lord. Therefore, as converts, those who have accepted Jesus Christ as their Lord and Savior, it is crucial for us to comprehend the mystery of God that Jesus Christ executed, along with the love inherent in that mystery. Through this understanding, we recognize that God now accepts us all as His beloved.

We are the modern-day tabernacle

Romans 12:1-2 says, "I beseech you therefore brethren that ye present your bodies a living sacrifice holy and acceptable which is your reasonable service. And be not conformed to this world but be transformed by the renewing of your mind that you may prove what is that good and acceptable and perfect will of God."

Whew! That is quite a mouthful, but from those two aforementioned scriptures, we can see that we are constantly offering unto the Lord the incense of our soul, and it is our job to offer acceptable sacrifices.

Romans 5:5

> *and hope maketh not ashamed; because the love of God is shed abroad in our hearts by the Holy Ghost which is given unto us.*

To reiterate, just as King Solomon offered his love in offerings unto the Lord, the love of God is in our hearts and our lives are those altars which are a precious gift and awesome privilege to be able to pour our love back out to God.

Summing this all up, the cross was love. There is no greater love than that of a man who would die for a friend. We have received one of the greatest gifts we could ever possibly receive, and that is **THE LOVE OF GOD**, all surmised by the death, burial, and resurrection of Jesus Christ, and the sending back of His Spirit, the Holy Spirit.

As you read further in this book, 4D love is about exploring and recognizing the love that the Holy Spirit has deposited in us and pouring that love back to Him. We no longer have to kill animals and offer animal sacrifices at the tabernacle; the tabernacle now resides on the inside of us, and we offer our lives as a sacrifice. It is God's love that means we no longer have to go to a priest; He is our high priest, and we can experience His love and presence anytime we want. It is about our love being perfected by the Holy Spirit so that our sacrifices before Him are holy and acceptable, and that we may be filled with Him.

"Dear friends, let us love one another, for love comes from God. Everyone who loves has been **born of God and knows God**." 1 John 4:7

WHY 4D LOVE?

Let's start the conversation about 4D love off with our scripture base, which is Ephesians 3:17 - 19 KJV

> **17** *that Christ may dwell in your hearts by faith; that ye, being rooted and grounded in love*

Verse 17 lets us know that our belief in Christ is the seed that will give roots of love and will lay a strong foundation of love and that foundation will strengthen us inwardly.

Verse 18 reads as follows:

> **18** *May be able to comprehend with all saints what is the breadth, and length, and depth, and height;*

Before we proceed to verse 19, I want to bring out the word comprehend in verse 18. The Greek word for comprehend is **exischuó. It**

means to have strength enough. Phonetic Spelling: (ex-is-khoo'-o)
Definition: to have strength enough
Usage: I have strength for (a difficult task), am perfectly able.

Many feel they understand love. Love is so deep that you are always in a place of being strengthened for the task of love. You never know what love will demand of you. It always stretches to cause growth and evolution. Love is not always simple; it may have difficult requirements and will be very sacrificing. It may even cause suffering. It is only through this that you can begin to comprehend the depths of love.

Now let's explore verse 19.

> **19** *And to know the love of Christ, which passeth knowledge, that ye might be filled with all the fullness of God.*

The fullness of God in this scripture is that we may become a body wholly filled and flooded by God. How can we become flooded by God? Just as the tabernacle we spoke about in the intro, when our responses to people and situations, which are offerings to God, are pleasing and in accordance with His Word, God, who is love, now consumes the offering and floods our lives in response with His presence.

Let's now read Ephesians 3:14-19 in the Message Bible

> **14-19** *My response is to get down on my knees before the Father, this magnificent Father who parcels out all heaven and earth. I ask him to strengthen you by his Spirit—not a brute strength but a glorious inner strength—that Christ will live in you as*

you open the door and invite him in.
And I ask him that with both feet planted firmly on love, you'll be able to take in with all followers of Jesus the extravagant dimensions of Christ's love. Reach out and experience the breadth! Test its length! Plumb the depths! Rise to the heights! Live full lives, full in the fullness of God.

The scripture above is the basis of this lesson and the reason why this eBook is called 4D love. We are going to explore the four dimensions of God's love, which are breadth, length, depth, and height.

I want to share a scenario that God used in my life to teach me about the four dimensions of His love.

Prophetic Conversation

God's Glory and God's love

This conversation started one morning with my frustrations of being a new mom to my then 2-year-old and how breastfeeding a 2-year-old had been very challenging for me. I had a bad week and was operating in and practicing strife, for which I was repenting, saying, "Lord, I turn from this wickedness. I don't want to practice strife after You have purified me and helped me break the bonds of this off my heart and mind." Then this conversation comes up as I'm talking to God about everything, and He begins to speak with me about my daughter, Sara. He was reminding me of the challenges I faced with her from birth. She was harder to deal with than my other two children. God was revealing to me that He was stretching my love, patience, and grace through this child and how **love had to be tested and matured** in me. He was showing me how He uses relationships to do this, whether on the job, through family, marital, or whatever the relationship may be.

God was sharing with me about how you can't have the weight of God's Glory on your life without your love walk being tested. What does being tested mean? When we talk about being tested in the context of one's love walk, it means facing challenges and trials that scrutinize and refine your capacity to love. These tests are opportunities for growth and purification, allowing you to develop a more profound and steadfast love. In essence, undergoing tests in your love walk is a process through which your ability to love is examined, refined, and perfected, enabling you to carry the weight of God's Glory in your life.

This is where God began to reveal to me and elaborate on the dimensions of God's love as spoken about in Ephesians 3:14-19. **He was explaining the depths of His love** by saying,

"You cannot go to another level in glory without your love walk being tried by fire, purified, and perfected." The two go hand in hand.

An example of this is Job. Let's read Job 1:1-5 below, which speaks to Job's character.

> *1 There was a man in the land of Uz, whose name was Job; and that man was perfect and upright, and one that feared God, and eschewed evil.*

> *2 And there were born unto him seven sons and three daughters.*

> *3 His substance also was seven thousand sheep, and three thousand camels, and five hundred yoke of oxen, and five hundred she asses, and a very great household; so that this man was the greatest of all the men of the east.*

> *4 And his sons went and feasted in their houses, every one his day; and sent and*

called for their three sisters to eat and to drink with them.

5 And it was so, when the days of their feasting were gone about, that Job sent and sanctified them, and rose up early in the morning, and offered burnt offerings according to the number of them all: for Job said, It may be that my sons have sinned, and cursed God in their hearts. Thus did Job continually.

Now let's skip over to Job 3:25 which reads as follows:

For the thing which I greatly feared is come upon me, and that which I was afraid of is come unto me.

What was that thing Job feared? It was the fact that Job's sons would curse God, and he would lose everything (Job 1:5).

God is continuously working to refine aspects of our lives, and love is among them. In the verse above, Job expresses that the very thing he feared has now come upon him. Essentially, despite Job being morally upright, walking in integrity, and fearing God, there was a specific area of his life that faced a profound challenge—his love for God.

Fear is the absence of love, and anytime there is an aspect of us that needs purification and the refining fire of God, God takes us through tests and trials to perfect those things concerning us.

The Bible affirms that God examines the heart, and in Job's case, his devotion and love for God underwent a profound test. Job endured a trial that stripped him of everything, yet in the conclusion, God restored everything to him twofold. This testing of his love for God resulted in Job attaining a higher level of glory and promotion.

Job 42:10

> **10** And the LORD turned the captivity of Job, when he prayed for his friends: also the LORD gave Job twice as much as he had before.

Try to see this scripture through this lens: here is Job, broken. He has experienced a skin-eating disease, his children died, he lost all his wealth—he lost everything within this physical world. In this place of brokenness, he is still having to extend love to people who criticized and scrutinized him. His love for God causes him to still minister the goodness of God and extend mercy and grace to those who did not see God the same way. He prays for them, and God grants him double. Do you know what double means? God restored the glory of the Lord over Job's life, which was the initial covering that was on Job life before God allowed Him to be tested. The blessings were indicative of the covering of God's presence, which was the Glory of the Lord upon his life. God restored the Glory of God at a greater level through the double return he received.

To summarize, what Job encountered was this: This world operates within a framework of order and hierarchy, synonymous with spiritual death.

Love, in essence, is the means by which we find reconciliation with God. The adversary seeks to undermine our ability to love through brokenness, fostering an environment of fear. The god of this world employs fear as a tool, blinding us to keep us under the dominion of death. From this fear, numerous demonic entanglements arise.

The adversary's strategy is clear: to perpetuate fear, brokenness, and despair, hindering the generation of love in our lives. Love, however, stands as the prevailing force, enabling us to overcome the challenges and influences of the world. It is through love that we emerge victorious over the adversities that seek to dominate our existence.

I'm reminded of a Sunday in church when I was listening to a visiting Apostle's testimony of how her sister treated her so meanly while she was on her deathbed. God told this apostle that she had to love her sister and that she had to continue to care for her even when she hurt her badly with her words and responses. Out of that, God made her a millionaire because when the sister died, she left all her millions to the apostle. Though she was pressed hard to love and care for her sister while she was alive, another level of glory and promotion came out of it.

It also reminded me of Jesus and how He had to endure the cross for the crown and weight of glory that rests on Him. There was an ascension and promotion, but He had to endure one of the greatest trials of being perfected in love. He who knew no sin had to become sin. Talking about sacrificing love.

One of my spiritual mentors is known for this quote: "People aren't your problem; you are your problem." In other words, your love walk is not perfected; it isn't matured, and you must allow God to perfect those things concerning you.

Have you been challenged in a relationship to grow and mature in love? What did you learn from your test?

THE DIMENSION OF BREADTH

GATEWAY: SEEK

**Another dimension of love is breadth.
In the message Bible it states, "Reach out
and experience the breadth!"
What is Breadth?**
broad plain (1), width (2).

GATEWAY: SEEK

Let's start this dimension off by explaining what
a gateway is. God gave me this revelation
about man, which I speak more on in my book,
"Office of the Midwife". He said that man is a
dichotomy, meaning that man has the ability to
be on earth and seated in heavenly places at
the same time. This makes man dimensional in
nature because heaven is a dimension and
earth is a dimension, and we have the ability to
dwell in both places. In essence, what makes
man a dichotomy is that man is a dimension
and a gateway all at the same time. In light of
this revelation, we can grasp the need to
explore the gateways of the four dimensions of

love. At the end of every dimension, I will explore its gateway and how we can experience a greater outpouring of that dimension by going through the gateway.

The gateway of breadth is seek and let's explore that. I'm an IT girl, and I have a B.S. in Computer Information Systems. With this type of degree, you are expected to come out of school and pursue a job as either a programmer or a systems analyst. In one of the classes I took, the teacher taught about the different types of searches a computer does. One of those searches is called a breadth search. It is supposed to be the most comprehensive search a computer could do. When the computer searches for an item with this search, if it doesn't find what you are searching for, then it does not exist because this search is going to search every file in every directory on every drive. This is analogous to what the dimension of breadth is like. It is a wide search.

The breadth of God's love is one's ability to seek God. This seeking takes you on a journey of search. It is the measure by which one has the ability to receive deep revelation from God and to expand and expound on the Word of God. It involves seeing the Word through the proper lens and giving the correct amount of knowledge and glory as it is revealed.

Psalms 119:105

> **105** *Thy word is a lamp unto my feet, and a light unto my path.*

As you dive into the Word, the light of God begins to shine brighter within you, giving you the ability to see the Word from its pure place and original intent.

The dimension of breadth is the ability to search out God, to seek Him and find Him through illumination, revelation, and understanding that comes through the knowledge of the Glory of God. All of this means you will experience truth revealed at varying levels.

Jeremiah 29:13

> **13** *And ye shall seek me, and find me, when ye shall search for me with all your heart.*

My definition of seeking God with all your heart mirrors the pursuit of "all" as expressed in Jeremiah 29:13. Genuine understanding of love arises solely from this complete and wholehearted search. Out of love you will seek

God, out of love you will search for God, and out of love you will find God.

You cannot search through scripture and receive great revelation without love being purified within your heart. The enlightenment of your understanding comes about through sanctification and search.

What does that mean? Many times we come to God with ulterior motives. Our search for God isn't always from a pure place. When you offer a sacrifice unto God just to exalt yourself in some form or fashion, then your motives aren't pure, and that is how you can tell that the level of love operating inside you is still in the process of being perfected. When love has not been purified, meaning the love within you hasn't been tested and challenged by trials, tribulations, and relationships, there are oftentimes ulterior motives in our sacrifices unto God.

When love has not been subjected to God's perfecting, you will always see the Word through legalism and self. But if you have deep love, you can now understand the who, what, when, and why of the scriptures.

It is only through God's love that we understand the revealed knowledge of God.

Proverbs 25:2

> **2** It is the glory of God to conceal things, but the glory of kings is to search things out.

It is only through God's love that we understand the revealed knowledge of God. Through your search for God, great revelation comes that will establish your place of rulership in the spiritual and earthly realms.

Returning to the story of Job, as he was going through the test, he had to come into a greater knowledge of who God is. In his agonizing and questioning of God, here comes the revelation of God. God begins to ask Job (summarizing), "Do you really know who I am?" Even in his search for why this terror had come upon him, a revelation from God came.

Love is the knowledge of glory. It is love that causes you to understand when God speaks to you.

What are some recent revelations God has given you through His word?

How have you been transformed through that revelation?

THE DIMENSION OF HEIGHT
GATEWAY: Humility

Another dimension of love is height.

In the message Bible it states, "Rise to the heights!"

What is Height?

GATEWAY: Humility

Height is defined as heaven; dignity, eminence.
NASB Trans: a high position

Let's review *Daniel 2:20-22*

> *Daniel answered and said, Blessed be the name of God for ever and ever: for wisdom and might are his: And he changeth the times and the seasons: he removeth kings, and setteth up kings: he giveth wisdom unto the wise, and knowledge to them that know understanding: He revealeth the deep and secret things: he knoweth what is in*

the darkness, and the light dwelleth with him.

The above scripture is a prime example of only out of love will mysteries be revealed. The first thing that Daniel exclaimed was Blessed be the name of God for ever and ever. That was his love and worship to God. Out of His worship, he had a revelation of who God is.

The scripture says he removeth kings, and setteth up kings:

You cannot go into the high places of God without His love. Any position you occupy is His love towards us. This love is extended to us out of our obedience and surrender to Him.

Then the scripture says, " he giveth wisdom unto the wise and knowledge to them that know understanding:
He revealth the deep and secret things: he knoweth what is in the darkness, and the light dwelleth with him. "

What kinds of elevations and promotions have you had? These promotions and elevations are God's love towards you.

You can't have that type of understanding of God unless you have spent time with Him and have become acquainted with who He is. Not only did he rise to the heights, meaning he had heavenly encounters, he had also seen his God bring him out of tests like the lion's den. Those encounters always reveal who God is to us.

Let's also review *1 Corinthians 2:9-10*

But as it is written, Eye hath not seen, nor ear heard, neither have entered into the heart of man, the things which God hath prepared for them that love him. But God hath revealed them unto us by his Spirit: for the Spirit searcheth all things, yea, the deep things of God.

The scripture above is the epitome of the searching out of God. You can't even know what God has prepared for you without love. Through love, these things are revealed, and knowledge is given unto you. In other words, you can't even search for God and see Him properly without love operating because it is only by His Spirit that He reveals Himself.

"For what man knoweth the things of a man, save the spirit of man which is in him? even so the things of God knoweth no man, but the Spirit of God. Now we

have received, not the spirit of the world, but the spirit which is of God; that we might know the things that are freely given to us of God. Which things also we speak, not in the words which man's wisdom teacheth, but which the Holy Ghost teacheth; comparing spiritual things with spiritual. But the natural man receiveth not the things of the Spirit of God: for they are foolishness unto him: neither can he know them, because they are spiritually discerned. But he that is spiritual judgeth all things, yet he himself is judged of no man."

You will not be able to comprehend (Eph. 18 the difficult task) love except by the Holy Spirit living on the inside that His love to us for God is love.

Now I want to talk about one more way we rise to the heights of God's love: a practical application in day-to-day life. I had a situation at my former job where there was some communication between me and a coworker. Something I said agitated this particular person and caused them to make my life a living hell intentionally. So initially, my response to this attack was to retaliate. We spent many days fighting back and forth. However, after a while, it just became an intentional tearing down of who I was. This person literally set out to destroy me. My boss would go to the person's boss and say, "Please tell her to be nice to Nikki." It was just that bad. Everyone could see the attack and felt badly for me. Anyways, finally one day after much anxiety, I said, "I'm choosing to operate in love. I'm going to deal with this in the spirit." That meant I chose to "rise to the heights" and sit in my seat of authority in heavenly places with Christ. I literally went before the Lord and repented for everything I did to exacerbate this matter, and then I began to bind this scenario to the love of

God and bind my day and myself to the love of God. I shut the mouth of the roaring lion and humbled myself in the midst of great adversity. Now, this didn't happen overnight, but every day got better. The breakthrough began on this very day when she called me on the phone and said to me, "With work like yours, an entire institution would fall." I did not retaliate at all. I kindly said, "Okay, thank you," and we hung up. I told my boss what she said and moved on. Every day, I would pray, "I bind my day to the love of God, and I bind me and this person to the love of God." Then this scenario happened: I went to a meeting a well-known preacher had, and God gave me a word about the breaking of day. He said He was pleased with how I chose to walk in love and that my prayers have caused a breakthrough. From that day forward, she no longer attacked me, and we lived amicably. When my father passed away, she actually sent me flowers.

This type of rising to the heights is actually when man humbles themselves under the hand of the Almighty, He, in turn, exalts you. He causes your enemy to be at peace with you. Having humility, dying to one's selfish nature, embracing the love of God, and rising to the height of our God-given authority silenced the roaring lion. So we see in both scenarios the ability to operate in our place of authority by being humble.

When was a time when you had to humble yourself so that God would teach you about His love? What revelation did you receive?

THE DIMENSION OF DEPTH

GATEWAY: Worship

Another dimension of love is depth.

In the message Bible it states, "Plumb the depths!"

What are the depths?

GATEWAY: Worship

The word of God contains a scripture that says, "the deep calleth to the deep." This means that through Christ, we are connected to the Spirit of God. That connection calls to the deep in our spirit. What is "the deep" in our spirit? It is all of the plans and all that God fashioned and formed in us. God calls for the revealing of these mysteries at the appointed time of God. As we progress through this journey of life, the unveiling of the mystery of God is like a body of water. The entry of that water is shallow, but the further progression into the water is deeper and deeper. This depicts how our understanding of the love of God progresses through our journey of faith.

An example of this is one thing I saw in God's word so wrongfully: how in the Old Testament, God was very intolerant of sin. Most people, myself included, see this through the eyes of our shallow understanding of love and think God is such a mean God, but this was not the case.

We fell from the knowledge of God's Glory when Adam and Eve ate of the tree of the knowledge of good and evil. You cannot be a partaker of something pure and holy when you have become full of sin and holiness is not in you. Holiness has a standard, and when that standard isn't upheld, the result of that is death. That is not hate; that is the result of sin. So this was not an issue of God not loving us; this was an issue of our failure to receive.

As I mentioned earlier, the depths of God's love is the ability to be able to go from glory to glory as in *Proverbs 3:20*

> *By His knowledge the depths are broken up, and the clouds drop down the dew God decides what revelation to release, what manner of favor He should bestow upon us based on our dwelling in His presence and the fullness of our container.*

Let's now read *2 Corinthians 3:18,* which is another requirement to experience the depths of God's love in His glory.

> *18 But we all, with open face beholding as in a glass the glory of the Lord, are changed into the same image from glory to glory, even as by the Spirit of the Lord.*

You must have reverential fear of God to **plumb the depths of God in the spirit**. Without reverential fear, you can't deep-sea dive.

You can't even hear the word of God properly without love. It will always seem foolish to you if you lack love; you'll only perceive it through your mere understanding.

The depths of God have to be revealed unto you.

I had a scenario where I was afraid of thunder. In my prayer times in the past, God would try to speak to me through thunder, but I was so afraid that I would just tell Him, "stop, you're scaring me." One day, as I laid in bed, thunder came and I became afraid. God began to speak to me through it, saying, "Do not be afraid," and suddenly, I felt overwhelmed by His love come over me. He wanted me to know it was Him and He comforted me through this encounter with His love. For the first time ever, I was no longer afraid of thunder because I felt His love so strongly. I exclaimed, "Oh my God, I'm not afraid anymore." Love has to be revealed.

This example is a measurement of where my love began when I first started growing in God. It reveals the shallowness of my understanding of love, which in turn made me perceive God's love from a shallow groaning.

The heart is depicted as an exceedingly deep place, characterized by the moanings and groanings akin to Jesus in the Garden of Gethsemane. This deep place of travail represents great intimacy—a place where moanings lead to the formation of Christ within, shaping believers into the very character of

God and allowing them to shun the mere APPEARance of evil. This deep place is where one progresses from being a child of God to becoming His bride.

What has God revealed about His plans and purposes for you?

What transformative processes have you undergone, and are currently undergoing, that constitute God's sanctification process in your life, leading you to greater intimacy with Him?

THE DIMENSION OF LENGTH

GATEWAY: Space and Time

Ephesians 3:19. Another dimension of love is length.

In the message Bible it states, "Test its length!"

GATEWAY: Space and Time

This includes the kairos timing of God (the appointed time) coming into our chronological time and gifting us opportunities to accommodate love.

When we think of length we typically think of a measurement. When you measure a thing you are measuring it to accommodate it. You are trying to assess how long, how wide, how high something is so that it can be accommodated. This same thing happens in love. How far are you willing to go to accommodate love for someone? Would you donate a kidney? Would you embark on a spacecraft journey to the moon? Would you marry someone simply because you love them? What lengths are you prepared to take to accommodate love? Each day presents us with the space and time to seize opportunities to accommodate love. It enables us to transcend our daily expressions of love and step into the supernatural love of God. What is the supernatural love of God? Agape love.

What is agape love?
According to Biblehub.com

> **Cognate: 25** agapáō – properly, to prefer, to love; for the believer, preferring to "live through Christ" (1 Jn 4:9,10), i.e. embracing God's will (choosing His choices) and obeying them through His power. 25 (agapáō) preeminently refers to what God prefers as He "is love" (1 Jn 4:8,16). See 26 (agapē).

> With the believer, 25 /agapáō ("to love") means actively doing what the Lord

prefers, with Him (by His power and direction). True 25 /agapáō ("loving") is always defined by God – a "discriminating affection which involves choice and selection" (WS, 477). 1 Jn 4:8,16,17 for example convey how loving ("preferring," 25 /agapáō) is Christ living His life through the believer.

Agape love is not just a love that moves according to feeling or emotion, it is driven by rational and in accordance to what the Lord wills.

There was something so simple but so profound that God shared with me recently. I asked Him what is your love? He said, "Nikki, everything I say and do is my love towards you". Do you know why that is so? Because as the Bible tells us, God is love.
1 John 4:7-10

7 Beloved, let us love one another: for love is of God; and every one that loveth is born of God, and knoweth God.
8 He that loveth not knoweth not God; for God is love.
9 In this was manifested the love of God toward us, because that God sent his only begotten Son into the world, that we might live through him.
10 Herein is love, not that we loved God, but that he loved us, and sent his Son to be the propitiation for our sins.

1 Corinthians 13:4 states that charity suffers **long**.

In science, space is associated with the universe, and it is said that the universe has no end. Can you imagine a picture in your mind about time with no end? One could come to the conclusion that such an event is indicative of the existence of eternity.

The Bible puts it this way in John 15:13,

> *13 Greater love hath no man than this, that a man lay down his life for his friends.*

Because He laid down His life, we can enjoy the great benefits of His love and a better covenant that is foundationally built on God's love. It's a privilege that allows the redemption of mankind and secures our eternity.

In Ephesians 3:19, length is defined as the language used in shadowing forth the greatness, extent, and number of the blessings received from Christ. Out of this better and new covenant, we are a blessed people, experiencing the abundance of God's blessings because of His love for us. That is a great length, I would say. Just imagine a measuring tape and having to measure the length of

God's goodness—it would be endless, and that is the length of His love for us.

Take a moment to write out the blessings of the Lord in your life, your family's life, and in your locality. Now, look globally and write those blessings out as well. You will begin to experience the length of God's love.

CONNECT WITH THE AUTHOR

Instagram, Facebook, tiktok, youtube @kingdomgirlnikki
Web: http://kingdomgirlnikki.com
Prophetic Blog: http://lifegivingrhema.com

For booking inquiries please reach out Nikki Garcia
Ministries at: (561) 618-8275. You can also email us at
nikkigarciaministries@gmail.com

ABOUT THE AUTHOR

Nikki Garcia received salvation and the baptism of the Holy Ghost at a very young age. She is a prophet of God with a mandate to teach and train the bride of Christ about prayer and intercession. She fulfills this mandate through her ministry, Nikki Garcia Ministries. Additionally, she operates in the mountain of business and holds a Bachelor of Science in Computer Information Systems. She serves as the CEO of Shine Global.

Nikki is the wife of Alex Garcia and the mother of four beautiful children: Jeremiah, Angelica, Sara & Zoa.

UPCOMING EVENTS 24'

24 Hour Prayer for the Nation - May 2, 2024

Come be apart. Visit https://kingdomgirlnikki.com for more information.

Did you love *4D Love*? Then you should read *Office of the Midwife* by Nikki Garcia!

www.ingramcontent.com/pod-product-compliance
Lightning Source LLC
Chambersburg PA
CBHW071510130726
47997CB00006B/2472